Table of Contents

Special thanks to Jessey Roy for the cover photo.

This book is dedicated to Steve Laplante and Jessey Roy.

Stay young and play!

Unleashing the Thrill: Exploring the Realm of RC Cars

Introduction

Remote Control (RC) cars have captivated enthusiasts of all ages by providing a window into the exciting world of motor racing. These smaller-scale, yet intricately detailed vehicles, offer an exhilarating experience reminiscent of their full-size counterparts. Through this essay, we embark on a journey to unravel the charm and allure of RC cars, exploring their design, technology, and the joy they bring to both young and old alike.

Body:

1. Performance and Power

RC cars pack impressive performance and power within their compact frames. Advanced models boast high speeds, smooth handling, and innovative features. With powerful electric or nitro engines, these miniature marvels can reach astonishing speeds up to 70 mph. This ability to replicate real-world driving dynamics adds an element of excitement and realism that enthusiasts crave.

2. Aesthetics and Design

The attention to detail in the design of RC cars is nothing short of remarkable. Manufacturers strive to capture the essence of various iconic vehicles, ensuring that every minute aspect is accurately represented. From the sleek exteriors to the intricately crafted interiors, these scaled-down replicas are truly a sight to behold. Whether it be a classic muscle car or a futuristic rally car, RC cars embody the artistry and craftsmanship of their full-sized counterparts.

3. Technology and Control

A significant aspect of RC cars lies in the technology that fuels their operation. The advent of digital proportional control systems has

revolutionized the way these vehicles are maneuvered. Precise controls allow for effortless steering, acceleration, and braking, providing an immersive experience for users. In addition, advancements in wireless technology and battery capacity have eliminated the need for inconvenient wiring, allowing for seamless operation and enhanced range.

4. Skill Development

Engaging in the world of RC cars not only offers pure entertainment but also fosters skill development. Drivers must hone their hand-eye coordination, reflexes, and spatial awareness to navigate the miniature race tracks, conquer jumps, and anticipate their opponents' moves. The pursuit of mastering these intricate machines fosters discipline, patience, and a competitive spirit, making RC cars an ideal hobby for individuals of all ages.

RC cars offer an escape from reality, allowing individuals to indulge in the thrill of motor racing in the comfort of their own homes. Beyond being mere toys, these miniaturized vehicles represent the perfect amalgamation of performance, design, and technological prowess. From developing fine motor skills to nurturing a passion for engineering and design, the experience of engaging with RC cars is a multidimensional adventure that captivates young and old alike.

The world of RC cars reveals an intricate and thrilling subculture. Their performance, design, use of cutting-edge technology, and inherent skill development make them more than just remote-controlled toys. As enthusiasts continue to push the boundaries of innovation and design, RC cars remain a beacon of excitement, proving that the allure of motor racing can be experienced by anyone with a desire for speed and a love for precision machinery.

RC Car History

RC (remote control) cars have come a long way since their inception and have witnessed significant advancements in design and technology over time. Here is an overview of the evolution of RC cars:

1. Early Years (1960s-1970s):
   - In the 1960s, RC cars were mainly simple and basic toys with limited functionality.
   - They were often gas-powered, utilizing small internal combustion engines.
   - The remote control systems used crystals to match frequencies between the car and the controller, limiting the number of cars that could operate simultaneously.

2. Electric Power Revolution (1980s):

- The 1980s marked a shift towards electric-powered RC cars, which became more popular due to easier maintenance and quieter operation.
- Nickel-cadmium (NiCad) batteries were commonly used, providing improved power and longer run times.
- More advanced electronic speed controllers (ESC) were introduced, allowing precise control over acceleration and braking.

3. On-road vs. Off-road Distinction (1990s):
- In the 1990s, RC cars began to split into two main categories: on-road and off-road.
- On-road cars, designed for pavement use, became increasingly sleek and aerodynamic, aiming for high speeds and cornering stability.

- Off-road cars, for rough terrains, saw advancements in suspension systems, tire designs, and improved torque and durability.

4. Digital Technology and Microelectronics (2000s):
- The 2000s brought significant advancements through the integration of digital technology and microelectronics.
- Traditional analog radio systems were upgraded to 2.4GHz spread spectrum systems, offering greater range, reduced interference, and the ability to accommodate multiple RC vehicles at once.
- Motors became more efficient and powerful, offering higher top speeds and acceleration.
- Lightweight materials like carbon fiber, aluminum, and graphite were utilized to improve durability and reduce weight.

5. Brushless Motors and Lithium Polymer Batteries (2010s-present):
   - Brushless motors replaced brushed motors, offering more power, longer lifespan, and improved efficiency.
   - Lithium polymer (LiPo) batteries became the standard, providing higher energy density, longer run times, and faster charging.
   - Electronic stability control (ESC) systems became increasingly sophisticated, offering enhanced stability and control for better handling.

6. Integrated Smart Features (present day):
   - Current advancements include integrated smart features in RC cars, such as Wi-Fi and Bluetooth connectivity, allowing for smartphone control and real-time telemetry data.
   - Some models have built-in cameras that stream live video to smartphones or virtual reality (VR) goggles for a first-person view (FPV) driving experience.
   - Advanced suspension systems, adjustable ride heights, and customizable settings for different terrains offer increased versatility.

Overall, the design and technology of RC cars have evolved from basic, gas-powered toys to high-performance, digitally controlled machines with improved speed, power, durability, and connectivity.

There are several key features to consider when choosing a beginner RC car. Here are some important factors to look for:

1. Durability: Beginner RC cars often experience crashes and collisions while learning to control them. It's essential to choose a car that is built with durable

materials, such as strong plastics or metal components, to withstand impacts and rough handling.

2. Ready-to-run (RTR): Look for an RC car that is labeled as "Ready-to-Run" or "RTR." These models come fully assembled and include everything you need to get started, including a transmitter, battery, and charger. RTR cars are convenient for beginners as they eliminate the need for additional purchases or complex setups.

3. Electric Power: Electric-powered RC cars, particularly those with brushed motors, are generally more suitable for beginners. They are easier to maintain, provide smooth acceleration, and are quieter compared to nitro-powered cars. Electric RC cars also tend to be more affordable and require less technical knowledge.

4. Beginner-friendly Controls: Opt for an RC car with user-friendly controls, such as a simple transmitter or controller layout. Some models also offer features like proportional throttle and steering, which provide smoother control and better maneuverability for beginners.

5. Speed and Power: While it can be tempting to chase after high-speed RC cars, it's generally recommended for beginners to start with slower models. Slower speeds allow for better control and reduce the chances of accidents. Look for a car that offers adjustable speeds or a slower speed mode to help build confidence gradually.

6. Parts Availability and Support: Ensure that there is good availability of spare parts and support for your chosen RC car

brand. Accidents happen, and being able to easily find replacement parts will be important for repairs and maintenance.

Additionally, it's crucial to consider your specific interests, whether you prefer off-road or on-road driving, and your budget when selecting a beginner RC car. Taking these factors into account will help you find the perfect match for your needs and provide an enjoyable experience as you delve into the world of RC cars.

An excellent and affordable option for a beginner RC car is the "ECX AMP MT" by ECX. Here are a few reasons why it's a recommended choice:

1. Price: The ECX AMP MT is available at a relatively affordable price point compared to other RC cars in the market.

2. Durability: It is built with a sturdy construction that can withstand beginner-level crashes and impacts. The ECX AMP MT's chassis and suspension components are designed to handle rough terrains and occasional collisions.

3. Ready-to-Run (RTR): The ECX AMP MT comes as a complete ready-to-run package, including a 2.4GHz transmitter, rechargeable battery, and charger. This means you can start driving right out of the box without any additional purchases or setups.

4. Electric Power: The ECX AMP MT is electric-powered, making it easy to operate and maintain for a beginner. Electric RC cars tend to be quieter, more affordable, and require less technical knowledge compared to nitro-powered models.

5. Beginner-friendly Controls: It features a simple and intuitive transmitter layout, providing easy control over speed and steering. The proportional throttle and steering allow for smoother maneuverability as you learn to handle the car.

6. Parts Availability: ECX typically offers good availability of spare parts, making it easier for you to find replacements in case of any accidents or wear and tear.

Remember, affordability is subjective, so it's best to check the current prices and availability in your local market or online retailers. Nonetheless, the ECX AMP MT offers a good balance of features, durability, and affordability, making it a solid choice for beginners eager to start their RC car journey.

RC Car Fun

Remote-controlled (RC) cars have been a source of joy and amusement for both young and old alike. The joy of racing these miniature vehicles across various terrains and performing daring stunts never fails to captivate the imagination. Despite their diminutive size, RC cars offer endless possibilities for entertainment and enjoyment.

One of the most exciting aspects of RC cars is the ability to race them. Whether on specially designed tracks or makeshift courses around the neighborhood, the thrill of competing against friends and family members is unparalleled. The precise control offered by the remote allows drivers to showcase their skills and navigate tricky obstacles with ease. The sheer excitement of a close race, with cars whizzing past one another, is sure to bring a smile to anyone's face.

Furthermore, RC cars offer the opportunity to engage in the art of customization. Enthusiasts can modify their cars with different tires, paint schemes, and even additional accessories. This personal touch allows individuals to showcase their creativity and uniqueness. With a wide array of aftermarket parts available, the possibilities for customization are virtually endless. This aspect of RC cars not only enhances the appearance but also enables enthusiasts to fine-tune their vehicle's performance to their liking.

Another dimension of RC cars is the ability to perform thrilling stunts. From high jumps to gravity-defying flips, these miniature vehicles can mimic the

acrobatic feats of their full-sized counterparts. The thrill of successfully executing a daring stunt is incredibly gratifying and adds an element of excitement to RC car fun.

The joy and fun derived from RC cars cannot be overstated. Whether it is the adrenaline rush of racing, the creative outlet of customization, or the thrill of performing stunts, these tiny cars offer endless entertainment possibilities. No matter one's age or skill level, the world of RC cars encompasses a sense of excitement and pure enjoyment that will continue to captivate enthusiasts for generations to come.

Popular Models

There are several popular RC car models and brands known for providing an enjoyable and fun experience. Some of the most popular ones include:

1. Traxxas: Traxxas is a well-known brand in the RC car industry and offers a wide range of models suitable for beginners to advanced users. Some popular models include the Traxxas Slash, Rustler, and Stampede.

2. Redcat Racing: Redcat Racing is another popular brand known for its affordable and durable RC cars. Models like the Redcat Racing Lightning EPX and Volcano EPX have gained popularity among enthusiasts.

3. Axial: Axial is known for its high-quality RC rock crawlers and trail trucks. Models like the Axial SCX10 II and Axial Wraith provide a realistic off-road experience.

4. Team Associated: Team Associated is a renowned brand in the RC racing world. They offer a range of models like the Team

Associated B6 and Team Associated RC10T6.1, designed for competitive racing.

5. Losi: Losi manufactures both gas-powered and electric RC cars, catering to beginners and experienced users. The Losi Tenacity series and Losi 22 series are popular among RC enthusiasts.

6. HPI Racing: HPI Racing offers a variety of RC cars, including drift cars, touring cars, and monster trucks. The HPI E10 and HPI Sprint series are well-regarded for their performance and durability.

Remember, the enjoyment and fun experience vary based on personal preferences and interests. It's always recommended to research and choose a model that suits your specific needs.

When looking for RC cars to ensure a high level of entertainment and enjoyment during usage, there are several features and specifications to consider. Here are some key ones:

1. Speed and Power: Look for RC cars with high-speed capabilities and powerful motors. Faster cars can provide a thrilling experience, especially for racing and off-road adventures.

2. Durability: A sturdy and durable construction is crucial, especially if you plan to drive your RC car outdoors or engage in rough terrains. Look for materials like high-quality plastic or metal chassis that can withstand crashes and bumps.

3. Off-Road Capabilities: If you want to take your RC car on off-road adventures, ensure it has features like rugged tires, suspension systems, and high ground clearance, which can enhance its performance on uneven surfaces.

4. Control Range and Frequency: Consider the control range and frequency of the RC car. A longer control range allows for more versatility, and multiple frequency options enable you to race with friends without interference.

5. Battery Life and Charging: Check the battery life and charging times. Opt for RC cars with longer run times and quick charging capabilities, as it reduces downtime between sessions.

6. Remote Control Features: Look for an ergonomic and easy-to-use remote control with intuitive controls. Some advanced RC cars may have additional features like proportional steering and throttle, multiple speed settings, and programmable options.

7. Realistic Design: Aesthetics play a significant role in the enjoyment of RC cars. Seek out models that closely resemble real-life vehicles, as the visual appeal enhances the overall experience.

8. Upgradeability: Consider if the RC car allows for upgrades and customization. Being able to modify and enhance your car's capabilities over time can keep the entertainment level high.

9. Special Features: Some RC cars come with additional features like LED lighting, sound effects, adjustable suspensions, or even cameras for a first-person view (FPV) experience. Such features can add extra excitement and enjoyment.

10. Accessibility: Finally, choose an RC car that suits your skill level, whether you're a beginner or an experienced enthusiast. Some models offer different modes for various skill levels, ensuring that everyone can have fun.

Remember, personal preferences may vary based on your intended usage, so consider these aspects to find the perfect RC car that matches your entertainment needs.

Building an RC Car

Building a remote-controlled (RC) car is an engaging and challenging endeavor that requires meticulous planning, technical skills, and a commitment to craftsmanship. This task necessitates a thorough understanding of various engineering principles and components, as well as careful consideration of the desired specifications and functionalities of the vehicle.

The first step in building an RC car is to identify the purpose of the design. This includes determining whether the car will be used for speed racing, off-roading, or simply for leisurely drives. Once the purpose is established, one must select suitable components, such as the chassis, motor, remote controller, and batteries, in order to optimize performance and durability.

After acquiring the necessary components, the assembly process begins with the construction of the chassis. This structural frame serves as the foundation for all other components, ensuring stability and balance while accommodating various functional parts. Attention to detail is crucial during assembly, as any misalignment can detrimentally affect the car's overall performance.

Next, one must install the motor and connect it to a power source, usually a set of batteries. Depending on the desired speed and torque, different types of motors can be selected to meet specific requirements. Additionally, choosing the right remote controller is essential to maintain precision and control while operating the car.

Finally, after ensuring all components are securely connected, it is time to test the RC car. This involves adjusting the suspension, aligning the wheels, and fine-tuning any other mechanical aspects to optimize its performance. If necessary, modifications can be made to the car's design, allowing for further improvements and personalization.

Building an RC car demands dedication, precision, and an understanding of engineering principles. The process provides a valuable opportunity to develop technical skills, ignite creativity, and experience the joy of constructing a functional vehicle. With patience and perseverance, one can create an RC car that not only brings satisfaction but also offers countless hours of enjoyment.

Building an RC car from scratch requires several essential components. These components may vary depending on the specific type of RC car, but here are the common essential components:

1. Chassis: The chassis is the structural frame that holds all the components together. It provides stability and support for the other parts.

2. Power source: A power source is required to run the RC car. Most RC cars use rechargeable batteries. For small RC cars, often a single lithium polymer (LiPo) battery is used, while larger cars may require multiple battery packs or even gasoline engines.

3. Motor and ESC: The motor is responsible for generating power to move the RC car. An Electronic Speed Controller (ESC) is used to control the motor's speed and direction.

4. Radio system: The radio system consists of a transmitter and a receiver. The transmitter is held by the user and sends control signals to the receiver mounted on the RC car. These signals control the car's movements like forward, backward, left, and right.

5. Steering system: The steering system is responsible for turning the RC car. It usually consists of a servo motor connected to the front wheels to control their direction.

6. Suspension system: The suspension system allows the RC car to absorb shocks and handle rough terrains. It typically includes springs, shock absorbers, and suspension arms.

7. Wheels and tires: The wheels provide the car's contact with the ground, and the tires provide traction. They should be chosen based on the type of terrain the RC car will be used on, such as off-road or on-road.

8. Gear system: The gear system transfers the motor's power to the wheels. It consists of gears, differentials, and a drivetrain.

9. Body shell: The body shell provides the outer appearance of the RC car and protects the internals. It can be made from plastic, polycarbonate, or fiberglass.

10. Optional accessories: Depending on the desired functionality, additional components can be added, such as lights, sound systems, cameras, or sensors.

These components provide the basic framework for building an RC car, but the complexity and specific parts needed will depend on the builder's preferences and the type of RC car being built.

There are generally three types of motors that are commonly used in building an RC car from scratch:

1. Brushed DC Motors: These motors are one of the most commonly used types in RC cars. They are affordable, simple to control, and relatively easy to maintain. Brushed motors use brushes and a commutator to deliver power to the motor's rotating armature.

2. Brushless DC Motors: Brushless motors are becoming more popular in the RC car world due to their improved efficiency and power. These motors do not have

brushes, making them more durable and requiring less maintenance. They typically offer higher speeds and better acceleration compared to brushed motors.

3. Nitro/Gasoline Engines: While electric motors are more prevalent, some RC car enthusiasts still prefer nitro or gasoline-powered engines. These engines burn fuel to generate power and provide a real engine sound and exhaust emissions. Nitro engines require frequent tuning and maintenance but offer higher speeds and longer run times.

The choice of motor depends on factors such as budget, performance requirements, and personal preferences.

Brushless motors generally outperform brushed motors in terms of both performance and durability in DIY RC car projects.

Performance:

1. Power: Brushless motors provide higher power output compared to brushed motors. They have better torque and acceleration, allowing the RC car to achieve higher speeds.

2. Efficiency: Brushless motors are more efficient due to their design. They have less internal resistance, resulting in less power loss and longer run times.

3. Speed control: Brushless motors offer precise and smooth speed control. They can accelerate and decelerate quickly, enabling better control over the RC car's speed.

Durability:

1. Heat dissipation: Brushless motors are designed to dissipate heat more effectively compared to brushed motors. This helps prevent overheating, which can damage the motor.

2. Brushes and commutators: Brushless motors do not have brushes and commutators that wear out over time. The absence of these mechanical components increases the overall durability and lifespan of the motor.

3. Maintenance: Brushless motors require less maintenance compared to brushed motors. Brush changes and commutator cleaning, common tasks for brushed motors, are not necessary for brushless motors.

Brushless motors offer superior performance and durability compared to brushed motors in DIY RC car projects. Although they are generally more expensive, their higher efficiency and longer lifespan make them a preferred choice for RC car enthusiasts.

There are several advantages and disadvantages of using brushless motors over brushed motors for DIY RC car projects in terms of performance and long-term durability:

Advantages of brushless motors:

1. Higher Efficiency: Brushless motors are more efficient than brushed motors, which means they convert more electrical energy into mechanical power. This efficiency reduces power loss and allows for longer running times.

2. Higher Power Output: Brushless motors generally have higher power output and torque, resulting in increased speed and acceleration. This is particularly advantageous for RC car projects that require high performance.

3. Longer Lifespan: Since brushless motors don't have brushes that wear out over time, they typically have a longer lifespan and require less maintenance. This can save money on replacement parts and reduce downtime for repairs.

4. Smoother Operation: Brushless motors provide smoother and more consistent power delivery due to the absence of brushes and commutators. This results in improved vehicle control and a more enjoyable driving experience.

Disadvantages of brushless motors:

1. Cost: Brushless motors are generally more expensive than brushed motors. The initial investment for a brushless motor setup can be higher, including the cost of the motor, electronic speed controller (ESC), and compatible batteries.

2. More Complex Electronics: Brushless motors require an electronic speed controller (ESC) to control their operation, which adds complexity to the system compared to the simple design of brushed motors. This may require additional technical knowledge and troubleshooting skills during installation and maintenance.

3. Limited Compatibility: Brushless motors often require specific ESCs and batteries to operate optimally. Choosing the right combination of components can be crucial

for achieving the desired performance, and not all brushless motors may be compatible with every RC car chassis.

4. Voltage Sensitivity: Brushless motors are often more sensitive to voltage fluctuations, requiring consistent and

appropriate power supply to prevent damage. This sensitivity means additional attention should be given to selecting the correct batteries and voltage regulators.

Considering these advantages and disadvantages can help inform the decision between brushed and brushless motors for a DIY RC car project, depending on individual preferences and requirements.

Remotes: Revolutionizing the World of Remote Control Cars

When it comes to remote control cars, there is no denying that the remote plays a crucial role in controlling the vehicle's movements. Over the years, technological advancements have significantly improved the functionality and usability of RC car remotes, transforming the hobby into an immersive and exciting experience for hobbyists of all ages. In this essay, we will explore the various features and advancements of RC car remotes that have revolutionized the world of remote control cars.

The evolution of RC car remotes can be traced back to their humble beginnings, where simple joysticks or buttons were used to control basic forward, backward, left, and right movements. However, with the advancements in technology, modern RC car remotes have become much more sophisticated. One of the significant improvements is the inclusion of proportional control, allowing users to have precise control over the speed

and direction of their RC cars. This feature enables hobbyists to perform intricate maneuvers and enhance their overall driving experience.

Another breakthrough in RC car remote technology is the introduction of digital proportional radios. These remotes use digital signals instead of analog ones, resulting in better signal precision and reduced interference from other devices. Digital proportional radios provide a more reliable and responsive connection between the remote and the RC car, allowing for seamless control and eliminating lag or latency issues. Furthermore, digital radios often offer increased range, making it easier for users to operate their RC cars in larger areas.

In recent years, smartphone integration has become a popular addition to RC car remotes. With the help of compatible mobile applications, users can control their RC cars through their smartphones. This innovation brings a new level of convenience and versatility to the hobby, as it combines easily accessible touchscreens with the power of traditional remote controls. Additionally, smartphone integration opens up possibilities for additional features like GPS tracking, live camera feeds, and augmented reality overlays, enhancing the user's RC car experience even further.

The ergonomics and design of RC car remotes have also undergone significant improvements. Manufacturers now prioritize comfort, ensuring that remotes are comfortable to hold and operate for extended periods. Additionally, the inclusion of ergonomic buttons and control layouts enhances the user's ability to perform precise movements effortlessly. Some remotes even feature backlit buttons or customizable settings, catering to the preferences and needs of individual users.

RC car remotes have come a long way since their inception, undergoing notable advancements that have revolutionized the world of remote control cars. The introduction of proportional control, digital proportional radios, smartphone integration, and improved ergonomics has transformed remote control car driving into an immersive and enjoyable experience. As technology continues to evolve, we can only anticipate further innovations in RC car remotes, enhancing the hobby's appeal and pushing its boundaries even further.

There are several different types of RC car remotes available in the market, including:

1. Pistol Grip Remotes: These are the most common type of RC car remote. They have a pistol-like grip with a trigger to control the throttle and a wheel or joystick for steering.

2. Stick Remotes: Stick remotes are similar to pistol grip remotes, but instead of a pistol-like grip, they have two sticks—one for throttle control and another for steering.

3. Wheel Remotes: These remotes have a steering wheel similar to a real car's steering wheel. They also usually have a trigger for throttle control.

4. Gamepad Remotes: Some RC car remotes resemble game controllers, with buttons and joysticks for controlling throttle and steering.

5. Smartphone App Remotes: Many modern RC cars can be controlled using a smartphone app. These apps usually utilize

the smartphone's touch screen for controlling the car's movements.

6. Computer Transmitters: These remotes are used for advanced RC car models and are typically connected to a computer for precise control. They offer additional features, such as programmable settings and telemetry data.

7. Multi-channel Remotes: Multi-channel remotes allow you to control multiple RC cars at the same time, using different frequencies or channels.

It's important to note that the availability of these different types of remotes may vary depending on the specific RC car model and brand.

Transmitter: A Controller for Speed and Control

The thrill of operating a miniature vehicle wirelessly and maneuvering it with precision is an exciting experience. Behind the scenes, however, lies a key component that makes this seamless control possible - the RC car transmitter. In this essay, we will explore the functionalities and features of an RC car transmitter, highlighting its importance in providing speed and control to these miniature vehicles.

To understand the significance of an RC car transmitter, it is essential to delve into its basic functionality. The transmitter is a handheld device that wirelessly communicates with the receiver on the RC car, sending signals that dictate its movement. Think of it as the brains of the operation, responsible for instructing the car to go forward, reverse, turn left, turn right, or apply brakes. Without a transmitter, the RC car would be rendered motionless.

One of the most critical features of an RC car transmitter is its ability to control the speed at which the car moves. A well-designed transmitter provides proportional control over acceleration and deceleration, offering a smooth and realistic driving experience. By varying the position of the throttle trigger on the transmitter, the user can dictate the speed at which the RC car moves, allowing for precise control in different situations. Whether it's a high-speed race or navigating a tight corner, the transmitter ensures that the user can adjust the car's speed accordingly.

In addition to speed control, an RC car transmitter also allows for precise steering control. This is achieved through the inclusion of a steering wheel or joystick on the transmitter. By manipulating the position of the steering control, the user can steer the RC car in different directions, enabling it to navigate obstacles or follow a specific path. The sensitivity and responsiveness of the steering control are crucial for providing accurate and reliable control over the car's movement.

Moreover, many advanced RC car transmitters come equipped with additional features to enhance the user's control. These include trim adjustments, dual-rate steering, and exponential throttle. Trim adjustments allow fine-tuning of the neutral positions for the car's throttle and steering, ensuring that the car does not stray off in unintended directions when in neutral. Dual-rate steering enables the user to adjust the sensitivity of the steering control, allowing for a wider or more precise turning radius based on the driving conditions. Exponential throttle adjusts the sensitivity of the throttle control, providing precise control over acceleration and deceleration.

The RC car transmitter plays a vital role in providing speed and control to remote-controlled cars. Its functionalities, including speed control, steering control, and additional features, grant users the ability to maneuver their miniature vehicles with precision and finesse. Whether enthusiasts are indulging in high-speed races or navigating challenging terrains, the capabilities of the transmitter ensure an immersive and enjoyable RC car experience.

When choosing a transmitter for RC cars, you should consider the following features:

1. Frequency: Ensure that the transmitter has a compatible frequency with your RC car. Common frequencies include 2.4GHz, 27MHz, and 75MHz. It is advisable to go for 2.4GHz as it provides better range and interference-free operation.

2. Channels: Determine the number of channels you require. Basic RC cars usually require only two channels for steering and throttle control, but more advanced models may need additional channels for features like lights, sound, or special functions.

3. Range: Consider the range of the transmitter. A longer range allows you to control your RC car from a greater distance.

4. Ergonomics: Check for comfort and ease of use. Look for a transmitter that fits well in your hands and has easily accessible controls. A well-designed transmitter will enhance your control and reduce fatigue during long sessions.

5. Durability: Ensure that the transmitter is well-built and durable to withstand rough handling and occasional drops. Look for features like rubberized grips or protective casing.

6. Compatibility: Verify compatibility with your specific RC car model. Some transmitters are designed to work with particular brands or models and may not be universally compatible.

7. Battery Life: Consider the battery life of the transmitter. Longer battery life means you can have longer play sessions without interruption. Some transmitters may also have rechargeable batteries, which can be more convenient.

8. Features and Programmability: Depending on your needs and preferences, consider additional features like adjustable trim settings, dual-rate steering, digital or analog controls, and programmability for customizing settings or fine-tuning control.

It's important to do thorough research and read reviews to find a transmitter that meets your specific requirements and offers a good balance of features and value for money.

The number of channels in an RC car transmitter directly impacts the control and versatility of the vehicle. The channels refer to the number of individual functions or controls that the transmitter can manage. These channels are often used to control various aspects of the RC car, such as steering, acceleration, brakes, lights, and other auxiliary functions.

With a higher number of channels, the control of the RC car becomes more precise and flexible. Additional channels allow for more customization options, giving the user the ability to fine-tune different functions of the vehicle. For example, a transmitter with more channels can include separate controls for front and rear steering, allowing for greater maneuverability and control over the car's turning radius.

Moreover, higher channel count transmitters can also support more complex actions and features. Some advanced RC cars include features like shifting gears, opening doors, or adjustable suspension, which require additional channels to be controlled effectively.

The number of channels in an RC car transmitter directly affects the control and versatility of the vehicle. Higher channel counts provide more precise control, increased customization options, and support for complex functions, enabling more advanced and versatile operation of the RC car.

Wheels: The Key to Thrilling and Efficient Performance

When it comes to the world of remote control cars, the importance of wheels cannot be overstated. Wheels are not just mere accessories; rather, they play a crucial role in determining the performance, handling, and overall experience of an RC car. In this short essay, we will delve into the fascinating world of RC car wheels, highlighting their key features and the impact they have on the driving experience.

Firstly, the material used in the construction of RC car wheels significantly affects their performance. Most wheels are made from durable and lightweight materials, such as plastic or rubber. These materials provide optimal traction on a variety of surfaces, ensuring smooth maneuverability and efficient acceleration. Furthermore, the flexibility and shock absorption capabilities of rubber wheels allow for improved stability and enhanced control, particularly when racing on uneven terrains or encountering obstacles.

Secondly, the design of RC car wheels also plays a crucial role. One essential consideration is the size and tread pattern. Smaller wheels allow for faster acceleration and increased top speeds, making them ideal for speed-oriented RC cars. Conversely, larger wheels provide better traction and control, making them suitable for off-road vehicles that traverse rough terrains. Additionally, the tread pattern determines the grip of the wheels on different

surfaces, and specialized patterns can optimize performance on various terrains, such as asphalt, dirt, or grass.

Lastly, the composition of the wheels directly influences their durability and longevity. High-quality RC car wheels are often designed to withstand intense driving conditions, including high speeds, sharp turns, and jumps. Reinforced sidewalls and rims provide increased rigidity and damage resistance, ensuring that the wheels can withstand rigorous use without compromising their performance.

The significance of RC car wheels in determining the performance and driving experience of remote control cars cannot be overlooked. From the material used to the design and composition of the wheels, each aspect plays a crucial role in achieving optimal performance and excitement. Whether it is the traction, handling, or longevity, investing in high-quality and appropriate wheels proves to be a fundamental step towards enhancing the thrill and efficiency of RC car racing.

There are several different types of RC car wheels available in the market, each with their own advantages and disadvantages. Here are some of the common types:

1. Rubber Tires:

   - Advantages: Rubber tires offer good traction on smooth surfaces and are typically durable. They provide good handling and control, making them suitable for various terrains.

   - Disadvantages: Rubber tires may not perform well on rough or off-road surfaces, as they lack sufficient grip. They can also wear out quickly on abrasive terrains.

2. Foam Tires:

   - Advantages: Foam tires are lightweight and provide excellent traction on smooth tracks. They provide good control and precision.

   - Disadvantages: Foam tires may wear out quickly and can be easily damaged on rough or abrasive terrains. They do not perform well on wet or dirty surfaces.

3. Off-Road Tires:

   - Advantages: Off-road tires typically have deep treads with aggressive patterns, providing excellent traction on rough and uneven surfaces. They are designed to withstand the rigors of off-road driving.

   - Disadvantages: Off-road tires may not offer optimal performance on smooth or paved surfaces. They can be noisier and produce more vibration compared to other types of tires.

4. Slick Tires:

   - Advantages: Slick tires have a smooth surface without any treads, resulting in reduced rolling resistance. This allows for higher speeds on smooth tracks and better handling around corners.

   - Disadvantages: Slick tires lack traction on rough or off-road terrains, making them unsuitable for such conditions. They may also struggle in wet or slippery conditions.

5. Drift Tires:

  - Advantages: Drift tires are made of a harder rubber compound, allowing the car to slide and drift around corners. They offer a fun and challenging driving experience for drifting enthusiasts.

  - Disadvantages: Drift tires do not provide much grip, making them less suitable for regular racing or off-road driving. They can wear out quickly on abrasive surfaces.

It is important to consider the specific terrain and driving style when choosing RC car wheels, as each type has its own strengths and weaknesses.

Suspension: Enhancing Performance and Control

In the world of remote-controlled cars, suspension plays a critical role in ensuring optimal performance and control. Just as in full-size cars, the suspension system in RC cars supports the weight of the vehicle, absorbs impacts, and keeps the tires in contact with the ground. This essay delves into the key components and functions of RC car suspension, highlighting its importance in achieving a smooth and stable ride.

The suspension system in an RC car primarily consists of several key components: shocks, springs, and linkages. Shocks, also known as dampers, control the movement of the suspension by absorbing vibrations and impacts. Their adjustable nature allows enthusiasts to fine-tune their RC cars according to varying racing conditions. Furthermore, springs complement shocks by providing support and allowing the car to effectively navigate rough terrains without compromising stability.

Linkages, such as arms and rods, connect the wheels to the chassis, transferring forces and enabling smooth movements. These linkages are adjustable, allowing users to modify their suspension geometry for enhanced handling and overall performance. Additionally, anti-roll bars can be employed to minimize body roll, improving cornering ability and reducing traction loss.

An effective suspension system enables RC car owners to achieve greater control over their vehicles. With the ability to adjust the suspension, enthusiasts can tailor it to their driving preferences and specific racing tracks. A softer suspension setup, for example, may be ideal for a bumpy off-road circuit, whereas a stiffer setup might enhance cornering prowess on a smooth track.

The suspension system in RC cars is crucial for their overall performance and control. Through the harmonious combination of shocks, springs, and linkages, enthusiasts can fine-tune their vehicles to overcome various obstacles and optimize their driving experience. Whether for recreation or competitive racing, a well-designed suspension system brings stability, maneuverability, and a smooth ride to these miniature yet impressive machines.

When designing the suspension system of an RC car, several factors should be taken into consideration:

1. Weight distribution: The weight distribution of the car affects how the suspension system handles different terrains. The

suspension design should be able to distribute the weight evenly to maintain stability and control.

2. Terrain: The type of terrain the RC car will be driven on is a crucial factor. Different terrains require different suspension setups. For example, off-road vehicles need more suspension travel and shock absorption to handle uneven surfaces, while on-road vehicles require stiffer suspension for better handling on flat surfaces.

3. Suspension type: There are various types of suspension systems available, such as independent suspension, solid axle suspension, and multi-link suspension. Each type has its own advantages and disadvantages. The intended use of the RC car and the desired performance should be considered when choosing the suspension type.

4. Suspension geometry: The geometry of the suspension system, including the suspension arms, shock absorbers, and linkage, greatly influences the dynamics of the car. Correct suspension geometry ensures optimal handling, stability, and traction.

5. Adjustability: Having an adjustable suspension system allows fine-tuning and customization of the RC car's performance. The ability to adjust the ride

height, damping, and spring rates enables optimal performance for different track conditions and driving styles.

6. Durability: The suspension system should be designed to withstand the anticipated stresses and impacts during operation. Choosing durable materials, such as hardened steel

or aluminum, ensures that the suspension components can withstand the rigors of off-road driving.

7. Aerodynamics: Although not as critical for RC cars compared to full-scale vehicles, aerodynamics still play a role in RC car design. The suspension system should be designed in a way that minimizes drag and air resistance to improve overall performance.

8. Cost: The cost of the suspension system components should be considered, as it may impact the overall budget of designing and building the RC car. Balancing performance and cost-effectiveness is essential.

By considering these factors, RC car designers can create a suspension system that provides optimal performance, stability, and durability for the intended use and racing conditions.

Body: Enhancing Speed, Style, and Functionality

The body of an RC car is not just about aesthetics; it plays a crucial role in defining the overall performance and capabilities of the vehicle. From sleek designs to durable materials, the composition of an RC car body can greatly impact its speed, style, and functionality.

One of the key elements that determine the performance of an RC car is its aerodynamics. A well-designed body can significantly reduce air resistance, enabling the vehicle to achieve higher speeds. Manufacturers meticulously analyze factors such as downforce, drag coefficient, and airflow patterns to create bodies that optimize speed and stability. A streamlined shape with strategically placed spoilers and vents helps improve traction and prevent lift-off at high speeds. By minimizing turbulence and maximizing downforce, a well-designed body ensures that the RC car can reach its full potential when zooming around the track or navigating off-road terrain.

Beyond performance, the body of an RC car also contributes to its style and visual appeal. With a wide range of options available, enthusiasts can choose bodies that reflect their unique personality and preferences. From iconic replica bodies that mimic real-world cars to futuristic designs and custom wraps, the possibilities are endless. The body of an RC car allows owners to express their individuality and stand out in a crowd of hobbyists.

Durability is another crucial aspect when considering RC car bodies. The material used must be able to withstand impacts and crashes without succumbing to damage. Polycarbonate has emerged as a popular choice due to its lightweight nature and high impact resistance. This material flexes rather than shattering, allowing the body to absorb energy and protect internal components during collisions. Additionally, the flexible nature of polycarbonate allows for intricate designs and easy customization. However, other materials such as ABS plastic or fiberglass offer their own advantages, depending on the specific needs of the driver.

Functionality is not limited to performance and durability; the body of an RC car also affects its maintenance and ease of use. Many manufacturers now incorporate removable bodies, making it easier to access internal components for repairs or upgrades. Quick-release mounts and snap-on body systems facilitate efficient swapping of bodies for different driving conditions or styles. Moreover, well-designed bodies provide ample space for electronic components, batteries, and other accessories, allowing for easy installation and customization.

The body of an RC car plays a pivotal role in enhancing its speed, style, and functionality. The careful consideration of aerodynamics leads to improved performance and higher speeds. Personalization options allow owners to showcase their unique tastes and preferences. Materials such as polycarbonate ensure durability and protection during crashes. Lastly, functionality is enhanced through accessible maintenance and customization features. As RC car enthusiasts continue to push the boundaries of engineering and design, the body will remain a critical component in the evolution of these miniature speedsters.

The most popular materials used for RC car bodies are polycarbonate, ABS plastic, and lexan. Each material has its own advantages and disadvantages:

1. Polycarbonate:
- Advantages: Polycarbonate bodies are lightweight, durable, and flexible, making them ideal for racing. They are also transparent and easily customizable with paint and decals.
- Disadvantages: Polycarbonate bodies scratch and crack easily compared to other materials. They require careful handling to avoid damage.

2. ABS Plastic:
- Advantages: ABS plastic bodies are affordable and relatively durable, making them suitable for beginners or those who

prioritize cost-effectiveness. They are also resistant to impact and provide decent protection for the internal components.
- Disadvantages: ABS plastic bodies might not have the same level of detail and realism compared to other materials like polycarbonate. They can be slightly heavier, which may affect the overall performance of the RC car.

3. Lexan (high-quality polycarbonate):
- Advantages: Lexan bodies have similar advantages to polycarbonate bodies, as they are lightweight, flexible, and customizable. However, Lexan is generally considered a higher-quality version of polycarbonate, offering better clarity and strength.
- Disadvantages: The main drawback related to Lexan bodies is the higher cost associated with their superior quality.

Overall, the choice of material for an RC car body depends on the user's preferences, budget, and purpose. Polycarbonate is commonly used for racing or customization, whereas ABS plastic is more suitable for beginner-level or cost-conscious users. Lexan offers a higher-end option for those seeking enhanced clarity and durability, but it comes with a higher price tag.

Fiberglass bodies for RC cars generally offer superior durability and impact resistance compared to other materials like lexan or ABS.

1. Durability: Fiberglass is known for its exceptional strength and stiffness. It is a reinforced composite material that consists of glass fibers embedded in a resin matrix. This combination provides excellent structural integrity, making

fiberglass bodies highly resistant to cracking, chipping, or breaking under normal operating conditions. In comparison, lexan and ABS bodies are generally not as durable and can be more prone to damage upon impact.

2. Impact Resistance: Fiberglass bodies are designed to withstand high-speed impacts and collisions better than lexan or ABS bodies. The rigid nature of fiberglass helps absorb and distribute the forces generated during crashes, minimizing potential damage. On the other hand, lexan bodies, being a type of polycarbonate plastic, are more flexible and tend to absorb impacts by flexing, which can lead to deformation or cracking under severe stresses. ABS bodies, while more rigid than lexan, are generally less impact-resistant than fiberglass.

It's worth noting that while fiberglass bodies offer excellent durability and impact resistance, they may be slightly heavier than their lexan or ABS counterparts. However, the weight difference is usually negligible in RC car applications, and the added strength of fiberglass compensates for any slight increase in weight.

Fiberglass bodies are often considered to withstand high-impact collisions and rough terrains better than lexan (polycarbonate) or ABS (acrylonitrile butadiene styrene) alternatives. While there is limited direct evidence or specific studies comparing these materials for every possible scenario, we can examine the properties of fiberglass, lexan, and ABS to understand their strengths and weaknesses.

1. Fiberglass:
Fiberglass is composed of fine fibers of glass embedded in a resin matrix, usually polyester or epoxy. Its key advantages include:

- High strength-to-weight ratio: Fiberglass is known for its exceptional strength, stiffness, and impact resistance, which makes it suitable for applications that require durability.
- Good energy absorption: Due to its composite structure, fiberglass tends to absorb and distribute impact energy, reducing the concentration of force on any specific point.
- Resistance to chemicals and corrosion: Fiberglass is generally resistant to chemical degradation and is not susceptible to rust or rot.

2. Lexan (Polycarbonate):
Lexan is a transparent thermoplastic with high impact resistance often used in applications like riot shields, safety goggles, or bulletproof windows. Although
not as commonly used for vehicle bodies, it is worth considering its properties:
- Exceptional impact resistance: Lexan is highly impact resistant, even more so than fiberglass or ABS. It is designed to absorb and disperse energy, making it difficult to fracture.

- Lightweight: Lexan has a notably low density, making it lightweight yet strong.
- Vulnerability to scratching: While highly resistant to impacts, lexan is prone to scratching, which can degrade optical visibility over time.

3. ABS (Acrylonitrile Butadiene Styrene):
ABS is a common thermoplastic known for its toughness and impact resistance. It is widely used in the automotive industry, particularly in components like bumpers or interior trims, rather than for entire bodies. Key points include:
- Good impact resistance: ABS provides reasonable impact resistance and helps protect against minor collisions.
- Less rigid compared to fiberglass: ABS is more flexible and less rigid than fiberglass. It may be prone to deformation or cracking under severe stress.

- Vulnerability to temperature extremes: ABS can become brittle in extremely low temperatures.

While there may not be direct evidence or extensive studies comparing these materials for all specific applications, the properties listed above suggest that fiberglass bodies generally exhibit higher strength and impact resistance than lexan or ABS alternatives. However, the choice of material ultimately depends on the specific requirements, design considerations, and intended use of the vehicle or application in question.

There are several documented real-world examples and case studies that demonstrate the superior durability of fiberglass bodies over lexan or ABS alternatives in high-impact collisions and rough terrains. Here are a few examples:

1. Dakar Rally: The Dakar Rally is one of the most grueling off-road races in the world. Many vehicles participating in this race use fiberglass bodies due to their excellent durability. Fiberglass bodies have proven to withstand the high-speed impacts, rough terrains, and extreme conditions encountered during the race.

2. Monster Trucks: Monster trucks are famous for their ability to crush and jump over cars, buses, and other obstacles. These trucks often use fiberglass bodies because they can withstand the repeated impacts and heavy abuse. Fiberglass bodies have proven to be highly durable under extreme conditions and collisions encountered in monster truck shows.

3. Off-road racing: Fiberglass bodies are commonly used in various off-road vehicles such as rock crawlers and desert

racing trucks. These vehicles face challenging terrains, intense vibrations, and impacts. Fiberglass bodies have

consistently shown superior durability in these demanding environments, withstanding collisions, rocky terrains, and rough off-road conditions better than lexan or ABS alternatives.

4. Marine industry: Fiberglass is extensively used in the marine industry, particularly for boat hulls and watercraft bodies. Fiberglass provides excellent resistance to impacts, rough water conditions, and UV radiation. Its durability in marine environments is a testament to its ability to withstand harsh conditions.

While specific case studies and comparisons between fiberglass, lexan, and ABS alternatives may not be readily available, the long-standing use of fiberglass in industries such as motorsports, off-road racing, and marine applications demonstrates its proven durability and ability to withstand high-impact collisions and rough terrains.

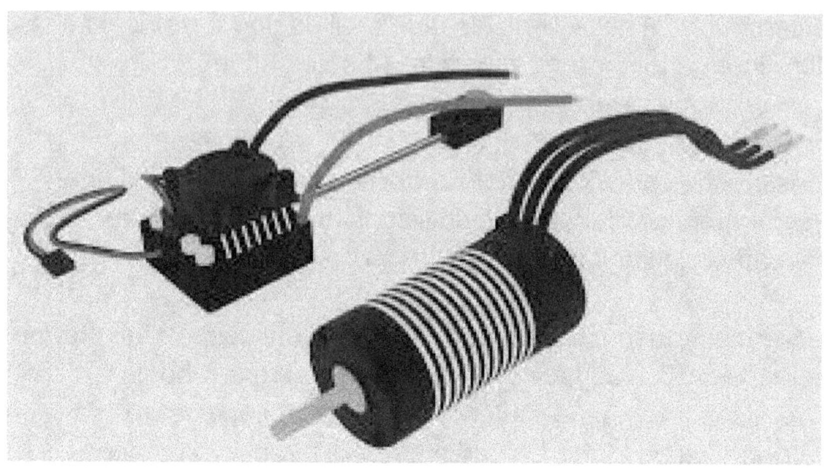

Motors: The Powerhouse Behind the Wheels

The heart of every RC car lies within its motor. A crucial component, the motor is responsible for translating electrical energy into mechanical energy, propelling the car forward with precision and power.

The most commonly used motor in RC cars is the electric brushed motor. This motor operates by passing an electric current through a series of wound wire coils known as the armature. These coils create a magnetic field, which interacts with permanent magnets located on the motor's outer casing. As the armature rotates, the magnetic fields push and pull against each other, causing the motor shaft to spin. This rotational movement is transferred to the wheels, enabling the car to move forward.

One advantage of brushed motors is their simplicity and affordability. With minimal components, they are relatively easy to build and maintain. The brushes, made of carbon or graphite, make direct contact with the commutator, an attached rotating cylinder. This contact creates friction, which results in wear over time. However, replacing the brushes is a straightforward process and ensures the motor's longevity.

Another popular type of RC car motor is the brushless motor. These motors operate on a completely different principle. Instead of using brushes and a commutator, they utilize a permanent magnet rotor and a multi-phase stator. When an electrical

current is applied, the stator's coils create an electromagnetic field that interacts with the permanent magnet rotor, generating rotational movement. Brushless motors are known for their efficiency and durability, as they eliminate the friction associated with brushed motors.

Brushless motors also offer higher speeds and increased torque, making them ideal for competitive racing. They have the advantage of precise speed control and can accelerate rapidly, giving RC car drivers an exhilarating

experience on the track. However, these motors tend to be more expensive due to their complex design and the need for additional electronic components such as a speed controller or ESC.

Within the realm of RC car motors, enthusiasts often choose between brushed and brushless based on their specific needs and budget. Beginners and casual hobbyists may opt for the economical brushed motor, while serious racers and enthusiasts seeking top-notch performance would undoubtedly gravitate towards brushless motors.

The RC car motor serves as the driving force, transforming electrical energy into mechanical power, enabling these miniature speed demons to conquer terrains with precision and agility. Whether it is the simplicity and affordability of brushed motors or the efficiency and high speeds of brushless motors, these miniature powerhouses are at the heart of every RC car, fueling the passion and excitement of enthusiasts worldwide.

When selecting a motor for an RC car, there are several key factors to consider:

1. Motor Type: There are two main types of motors for RC cars - brushed and brushless. Brushed motors are usually more affordable and require less maintenance, but they may have lower performance. Brushless motors, on the other hand, offer higher speed, power, and efficiency, but they are more expensive.

2. Voltage and Power Rating: It is important to match the motor's voltage and power rating with the capabilities of the car's battery and ESC (Electronic Speed Controller). You need to ensure that the motor can handle the voltage and power output of your setup.

3. Speed and Torque: The desired speed and torque of the RC car will determine the specifications of the motor. If you want a faster car, you'll need a motor with higher RPM (Revolutions Per Minute). If you need more torque for off-road or climbing purposes, you should opt for a motor with higher torque rating.

4. Size and Weight: The physical dimensions and weight of the motor should be compatible with the RC car's chassis and overall balance. It shouldn't add excessive weight or cause imbalance that could affect the car's performance.

5. Cooling and Heat Management: Consider the motor's cooling capabilities, such as whether it has built-in cooling fins or requires additional cooling methods like fans. Efficient heat dissipation is crucial to prevent overheating and motor burnout during prolonged use.

6. Compatibility: Ensure that the motor is compatible with the rest of the RC car's components, including the ESC, battery, and drivetrain. Check if the motor has the appropriate mounting options, connectors, and shaft diameter to fit your car's configuration.

7. Budget: Finally, consider your budget. Higher quality and performance motors often come at a higher price point. Determine your budget range and choose a motor that offers a good balance between performance and cost.

By considering these key factors, you can select a motor that meets your desired performance, endurance, and budget requirements for your RC car.

The ideal motor size and power rating for different types of RC cars can vary depending on several factors, including the size of the vehicle, its weight, the type of driving you plan to do, and personal preferences. However, here are some general guidelines for different types of RC cars:

1. Off-Road Trucks: Off-road trucks are designed to handle rough terrains such as dirt, gravel, or grass. They require powerful motors for efficient performance. A motor size around 540 or 550 with a power rating of 15-25 turns or 3000-4000kv should be suitable for most off-road trucks.

2. On-Road Cars: On-road cars are built for speed and smooth surfaces such as asphalt or concrete. They require motors that can provide high speeds and good acceleration. A motor size

around 540 or 550 with a power rating of 8-12 turns or 4000-6000kv is often used for on-road cars.

3. Drift Cars: Drift cars are designed for controlled slides and drifting maneuvers. They require a balance of power and control. A motor size around 540 with a power

rating of 8-15 turns or 4000-5000kv can provide a good combination of torque and speed for drift cars.

It's important to note that these motor size and power rating suggestions are approximate and can vary based on specific model designs, desired performance characteristics, and personal preferences. Additionally, the specific battery, speed controller, and gear setup also play a significant role in determining the overall performance of an RC car.

RC Car Safety

Remote-controlled (RC) cars have been popular among enthusiasts for many years. These miniature vehicles provide entertainment and excitement to both children and adults alike. However, it is important to consider safety precautions in order to enjoy this hobby responsibly and minimize potential risks.

First and foremost, it is crucial to operate RC cars in designated areas, such as parks or empty parking lots. These locations offer ample space to maneuver the vehicle safely, reducing the risk of collisions with pedestrians, other vehicles, or property. It is imperative to avoid public roads or crowded areas to prevent accidents and potential harm to others.

Furthermore, maintaining proper control over the RC car is essential. Most modern RC cars come equipped with speed control capabilities. It is recommended to start with lower speeds, especially for inexperienced users, as high speeds can make it difficult to react promptly to changes in the environment. Additionally, ensuring a clear line of sight between the operator and the RC car helps maintain control and avoid obstacles or potential collisions.

Lastly, utilizing the correct safety equipment is of utmost importance. Wearing protective gear, such as helmets and knee pads, can significantly reduce the risk of injury, especially when performing stunts or jumps. Additionally, it is essential to keep in mind the age appropriateness of the RC car model, as some advanced models may require a higher level of skill and experience.

In conclusion, while operating RC cars can be an enjoyable hobby, it is essential to prioritize safety to prevent accidents and injuries. By adhering to designated areas, maintaining control, and utilizing appropriate safety equipment, enthusiasts can participate in this activity responsibly and minimize potential risks.

When purchasing an RC car for a child, there are several key safety features to consider:

1. Age appropriateness: Ensure that the RC car is suitable for your child's age range. Many models have recommended age limits, which can help you choose an appropriate option that matches your child's abilities.

2. Speed control: Look for RC cars with adjustable speed settings, particularly for younger children. This enables you to limit the top speed of the car, making it easier for kids to control and reducing the risk of accidents.

3. Durability: Choose an RC car that is built to withstand crashes and rough play. Look for models with robust construction and quality materials that can handle the

occasional impact without breaking easily, reducing the risk of small parts becoming choking hazards.

4. Safety certifications: Check if the RC car has obtained any safety certifications, such as the CE mark or ASTM certification. These indicate that the product has undergone safety testing and meets certain standards for child use.

5. Remote control range: Consider the range of the remote control. Make sure it is sufficient for supervising your child's play without being too far away, which could increase the risk of accidents or losing control of the vehicle.

6. Easy to operate controls: Look for an RC car with user-friendly controls that are easy for children to understand and operate. Avoid models with complex or sensitive controls that may be difficult for young kids to handle.

7. Battery safety: Pay attention to the type of batteries used in the RC car. Rechargeable batteries are a good option, and ensure that they have appropriate voltage levels to avoid overpowering the vehicle. Additionally, make sure that battery compartments are securely closed to prevent access to the batteries.

8. Adjustable suspension: Opt for RC cars with adjustable suspension systems. This feature helps to absorb shocks and impacts, making the car more stable and reducing the risk of accidents and damage.

9. Avoid sharp edges or protruding parts: Ensure that the RC car does not have any sharp edges or protruding parts that could cause injuries.

Remember, adult supervision is crucial when children are using RC cars to ensure a safe and enjoyable experience.

RC Car Repair

RC cars are an exciting and popular hobby enjoyed by individuals of all ages. These miniature vehicles provide enthusiasts with endless entertainment and the opportunity to partake in thrilling races and challenges. However, as with any mechanical device, RC cars are not immune to occasional breakdowns or malfunctions. This necessitates the skilled art of RC car repair, which involves diagnosing and rectifying any issues that may arise.

The repair process for RC cars typically begins with a thorough examination of the vehicle. This involves checking the various components such as the motor, gears, suspension, and electronic circuits for any signs of damage or wear. Once the problem is identified, the next step is to gather the necessary tools and replacement parts required for the repair.

One crucial aspect of RC car repair is having a solid understanding of the vehicle's mechanics. This allows the repairer to disassemble the car with precision and locate the specific area requiring attention. Whether it is fixing a broken axle, replacing a worn-out gear, or soldering a loose wire, a keen eye and a steady hand are indispensable in successfully executing these repairs.

In addition to manual dexterity, knowledge of electronics is pivotal for efficiently resolving any electrical issues in an RC car. Understanding how the electronic components function and being able to detect faults in the wiring or circuitry is paramount. Moreover, staying updated with the latest advancements in remote control technology ensures that repairs are carried out in line with industry standards.

RC car repair is a skilled endeavor that necessitates a combination of mechanical and technical expertise. It not only requires a comprehensive understanding of the vehicle's mechanics but also the ability to diagnose and resolve any electronic malfunctions. A successful repair ultimately ensures that RC car enthusiasts can continue to indulge in their exciting hobby without interruption.

The physical design of RC cars has evolved significantly over time to improve aerodynamics, stability, and maneuverability. Some notable changes include:

1. Streamlined Body Shapes: One of the key changes in RC car design is the adoption of sleek and aerodynamic body shapes. Early RC cars had boxy designs, but modern models feature smooth and curved bodies to reduce drag and improve airflow.

2. Low Profile: RC cars are now designed with a lower center of gravity to enhance stability. Lower profiles reduce the car's susceptibility to rolling or tipping over during high-speed turns or maneuvers. The lowered center of gravity allows for better balance and cornering performance.

3. Spoilers and Wings: Many RC cars feature spoilers or wings on the rear to generate downforce, which enhances traction and stability. These aerodynamic elements help keep the car planted to the ground, especially during high-speed runs and aggressive cornering.

4. Splitter and Diffuser: Similar to full-scale racing cars, some advanced RC models incorporate splitters at the front and diffusers at the rear. These features help manage airflow and create more downforce, resulting in improved traction and better overall stability.

5. Adjustable Suspension: Modern RC cars often have adjustable suspension systems, allowing drivers to fine-tune the car's handling characteristics. Adjusting the suspension can optimize the car's stability, control, and maneuverability on different surfaces or track conditions.

6. Improved Tires: Tires play a crucial role in RC car performance. Over time, tire compounds, tread patterns, and sizes have been developed specifically for different surfaces. These advancements provide better grip, enhanced traction, and improved overall handling.

7. Enhanced Electronic Stability Control (ESC): Many high-end RC cars now come equipped with electronic stability control systems. These systems use sensors and intelligent algorithms to provide stability assistance during acceleration, cornering, and braking. ESC improves control and reduces the chances of losing traction or spinning out.

8. Advanced Steering Mechanisms: RC cars have seen improvements in steering systems, such as the introduction of ball bearings for smoother and

more precise steering response. Additionally, some models incorporate advanced servo motors and proportional steering systems, allowing for more accurate and responsive control.

9. Lightweight Materials: The use of lightweight materials like carbon fiber, aluminum, and composite plastics has reduced the overall weight of RC cars. This reduction in weight improves acceleration, maneuverability, and agility.

10. Improved Electronics: The electronic components in RC cars, such as motors, batteries, and electronic speed controllers, have also evolved. More efficient motors provide higher speeds, longer run times, and better overall performance. Additionally, advancements in battery technology have increased power output and reduced weight.

The physical design of RC cars has seen significant advancements to enhance aerodynamics, stability, and maneuverability. These improvements mimic the developments in full-scale racing cars and result in more thrilling and realistic performance for RC enthusiasts.

There are several design elements that have been incorporated into RC cars to improve stability during high-speed maneuvers:

1. Aerodynamic Body Design: RC cars with sleek, aerodynamic bodies are designed to reduce drag and improve stability at higher speeds. They often feature curves, spoilers, and diffusers to optimize airflow and reduce lift.

2. Wide Tires: RC cars designed for high-speed maneuvers typically have wider tires. These tires offer increased traction and help maintain stability during turns and acceleration.

3. Low Center of Gravity: Cars with a lower center of gravity tend to be more stable during high-speed maneuvers. RC cars achieve this by placing heavy components like the battery and motor as low as possible, or designing the chassis to sit closer to the ground.

4. Adjustable Suspension System: High-speed RC cars often come with adjustable suspension systems, allowing users to fine-tune the car's responses to different terrains and driving conditions. A well-tuned suspension can enhance stability by keeping the tires in constant contact with the ground.

5. Stiff Chassis: A rigid or stiff chassis helps to reduce flex during high-speed maneuvers, providing better control and stability. RC cars designed for speed often incorporate carbon fiber or aluminum components to enhance structural rigidity.

6. Countersteering Systems: Some high-performance RC cars employ countersteering systems that automatically adjust the steering angle of the front wheels based on speed and traction conditions. These systems can help maintain stability during high-speed cornering.

7. Electronic Stability Control (ESC): Advanced RC cars may come equipped with electronic stability control systems. ESC uses sensors to detect and correct steering and traction issues in real-time, providing additional stability during high-speed maneuvers.

8. Differential Systems: Differential systems distribute power between the wheels during turns, allowing for better traction and stability. Limited-slip differentials or spools are commonly

used in high-speed RC cars to prevent wheels from losing traction and maintain stability during aggressive driving.

9. High-Speed Steering Servos: To maintain stability during high-speed maneuvers, RC cars require precise and responsive steering. Installing high-quality, high-speed steering servos provides better control and stability, allowing for precise maneuverability.

10. Higher-Power Motors: RC cars designed for speed often feature powerful motors capable of generating higher speeds. The increased power allows the car to maintain stability during acceleration and high-speed maneuvers.

These design elements work together to maximize stability and control in RC cars during high-speed maneuvers, ensuring a safer and more exciting driving experience.

Some of the most common issues faced while repairing RC cars include:

1. Battery and Power Issues: RC cars may have problems with battery charging, battery life, or insufficient power. To resolve these issues, try replacing the battery or charge it properly according to the manufacturer's recommendations. Also, ensure that the power connectors are clean and properly connected.

2. Motor or Engine Problems: Motor issues may result in poor performance or the RC car not moving at all. Check for loose wires or damaged motor parts and repair or replace them accordingly. Lubricating the motor or engine can also help improve its performance.

3. Suspension and Steering Issues: If the RC car is having difficulty turning or the suspension is not working correctly,

check for any loose or broken suspension parts. Tighten or replace the parts as needed and adjust the suspension settings to improve performance.

4. Transmission and Gearbox Problems: Transmission issues can lead to difficulties in shifting gears or the RC car not moving smoothly. Inspect the transmission or gearbox for any loose or damaged parts and fix or replace them accordingly. Lubricating the gears can also help in resolving any gear-shifting issues.

5. Electronic and Wiring Troubles: Problems such as loose wires, faulty connectors, or damaged electronic components can affect the overall function of the RC car. Carefully check the wiring, connectors, and circuit board for any issues, and repair or replace them as needed.

6. Body and Chassis Damage: RC cars may experience body or chassis damage due to collisions or improper handling. Repairing body or chassis damage involves replacing broken parts, reinforcing weak areas, or using appropriate glue or adhesives for repairs.

To effectively resolve these issues, refer to the RC car's user manual for specific troubleshooting tips provided by the manufacturer. Additionally, online forums, RC car communities, or specific RC car repair guides can offer valuable insights and solutions. Seeking help from experienced enthusiasts or professional technicians can also be beneficial in troubleshooting and repairing RC car issues.

When repairing RC cars, here are some common challenges encountered in terms of electrical and mechanical components:

1. Electrical Component Challenges:
   - Battery Issues: RC cars rely on batteries for power, and common challenges include dealing with dead or damaged

batteries, poor battery performance, or improper charging techniques.

- Electrical System Failure: It is not uncommon for RC cars to experience failures within their electrical system, such as faulty wiring, loose connections, or blown fuses. Diagnosing and fixing these issues can be challenging.

- Motor Problems: RC car motors can suffer from various issues, such as burnt-out brushes, overheating, or lack of power. Identifying the problem and replacing or repairing the motor can be demanding.

- Radio Frequency Interference: RC cars operate on specific frequencies, and interference from other electronic devices can disrupt their performance. Troubleshooting and eliminating interference can be tricky.

2. Mechanical Component Challenges:

- Suspension and Shock Issues: RC car suspensions and shock absorbers can wear out or become damaged, affecting the car's performance and handling. Repairing or adjusting these components can be a challenge, especially for complex suspension systems.

- Gear and Drivetrain Problems: Gears, gearboxes, and drivetrain components are often subject to high stress and can experience issues like stripped gears, loose belts/chains, or worn-out bearings. Replacing or repairing these parts can be time-consuming and require specific technical knowledge.

- Chassis and Bodywork Damage: During crashes or high-impact situations, the RC car's body or chassis may become damaged. Repairing or replacing these components can be challenging, especially when aligning or reinforcing them to ensure proper fitment and structural integrity.

- Tire and Wheel Issues: RC car tires can wear out, lose traction, or suffer from punctures. Repairing or replacing the tires and wheels, as well as balancing them properly, can pose challenges, especially for intricate wheel designs.

Repairing RC cars requires a combination of electrical and mechanical skills, troubleshooting techniques, and access to the right tools and spare parts. Additionally, staying updated with the specific RC car model's components and understanding its intricacies can help overcome these challenges effectively.

RC car enthusiasts can effectively address and resolve motor malfunctions or failures by following these steps:

1. Identifying the Issue: The first step is to identify the specific issue or malfunction. Whether it's a complete motor failure or just poor performance, understanding the problem is crucial.

2. Basic Troubleshooting: Perform some basic troubleshooting steps, such as checking the battery voltage, ensuring the motor connections are secure, and inspecting the gears and drivetrain for any physical damage or obstructions. Sometimes, minor issues can be fixed easily without needing to replace any parts.
3. Consult the User Manual: Check the user manual that came with the RC car for troubleshooting advice specific to your model. It may provide guidance on common motor issues and how to resolve them.

4. Seek Online Forums and Communities: Join RC car enthusiast forums or online communities where experienced hobbyists can provide insights and advice. Such communities often share their experiences and can help diagnose motor problems that others may have encountered before.

5. Contact Manufacturer Support: If the issue persists, it is best to contact the manufacturer's customer support. Most reputable RC car brands have dedicated support teams that can provide

assistance, troubleshoot the problem, and recommend appropriate solutions or replacement parts.

6. Replace or Repair the Motor: If all else fails, it may be necessary to replace or repair the motor. Depending on the type of RC car, motors are often replaceable. Online hobby stores, local hobby shops, or authorized dealers can supply the required motor or repair it if possible.

7. Preventive Maintenance: To avoid future motor malfunctions, regular maintenance is essential. Clean and lubricate the motor periodically, check the gears for wear and tear, and ensure the motor is not overheating. Regular maintenance can extend the motor's lifespan and prevent sudden failures.

Remember, each RC car may differ in terms of motor maintenance and troubleshooting, so it's crucial to refer to the specific manufacturer's guidelines and follow proper maintenance practices to resolve motor issues effectively.

Restoring the Thrills: A Comprehensive Guide to Repairing RC Cars

Remote-controlled (RC) cars have captivated enthusiasts for decades with their exhilarating speed, handling, and customization options. However, like any mechanical device, RC cars are prone to wear, tear, and occasional accidents. Understanding the fundamentals of repairing these miniature vehicles is crucial in ensuring their longevity and continuing enjoyment. This essay will delve into the Pastor framework – Problem, Analysis, Solution, Tactics, Outcome, and Review – to provide a comprehensive guide to repairing RC cars.

Problem:
The problem faced by RC car owners is the inevitable wear and tear that leads to malfunctioning or damaged components. Symptoms may include erratic steering response, engine failure, electrical problems, or broken body parts. Diagnosing these issues accurately is the first step toward finding viable solutions.

Analysis:
To effectively analyze the problem with an RC car, start by identifying the specific malfunction. For instance, if the vehicle is experiencing erratic

steering, examine the servo motor, steering linkage, or the receiver system. In cases of engine failure, focus on the fuel system, glow plug, or exhaust pipe. Electrical problems might relate to the battery, motor controller, or wiring connections. Lastly, broken body parts necessitate an inspection of the chassis, suspension system, or tires.

Solution:
1. Servo Motor Repair:
If the steering response is sporadic, check the servo motor for possible issues. Start by ensuring that the servo is securely mounted and the gears are not damaged. If the motor is not functioning at all, check for loose or damaged wiring, and test the receiver for a signal output. A replacement servo may be necessary if these steps do not resolve the problem.

2. Engine Failure:
In cases of engine failure, begin by inspecting the fuel system, particularly the fuel tank, fuel lines, and carburetor. Clean or replace any clogged parts, and ensure the fuel mixture and

needle settings are correct. Check the glow plug for cleanliness and proper functionality. Exhaust pipe blockages should also be cleared. If the engine still fails to start, consider a comprehensive rebuild or replacement.

3. Electrical Problems:
To address electrical issues, start by examining the battery for adequate charge and proper connections. Clean any corrosion on the contacts and ensure the motor controller is receiving a signal. Verify that all wiring connections are secure and replace any damaged wires or connectors. If electrical problems persist, consider replacing the motor or controller altogether.

4. Broken Body Parts:
For broken body parts, inspect the chassis for structural damage. Reinforce or repair any weak or broken areas. Inspect the suspension system, shock absorbers, and ball joints for damage, replacing any compromised components. Broken tires and rims can be replaced easily with available spare parts. If the damage is extensive, it may be worthwhile to consider upgrading to a more durable aftermarket body or chassis.

Tactics:
To execute these repairs successfully, one must be patient, meticulous, and have access to tools such as screwdrivers, pliers, wrenches, and adhesive

materials. It is also essential to consult the user manual and seek guidance from online forums or RC car communities for specific issues and recommendations.

Outcome:
Applying the problem analysis and implementing the corresponding repair solutions, RC car owners can expect a fully functional vehicle. Beneficial outcomes include improved performance, increased lifespan, and reduced costs associated

with repairs, as owners become adept at diagnosing and solving common issues.

The Pastor framework provides a systematic approach to effectively repair RC cars. By identifying the problem, analyzing its causes, applying appropriate solutions, utilizing the necessary tactics, monitoring the outcome, and reviewing the process, enthusiasts can confidently restore their RC cars to their former glory. By investing time and effort into these repairs, enthusiasts not only extend the lifespan of their beloved vehicles but also enhance their overall RC experience, ensuring countless hours of excitement on and off the track.

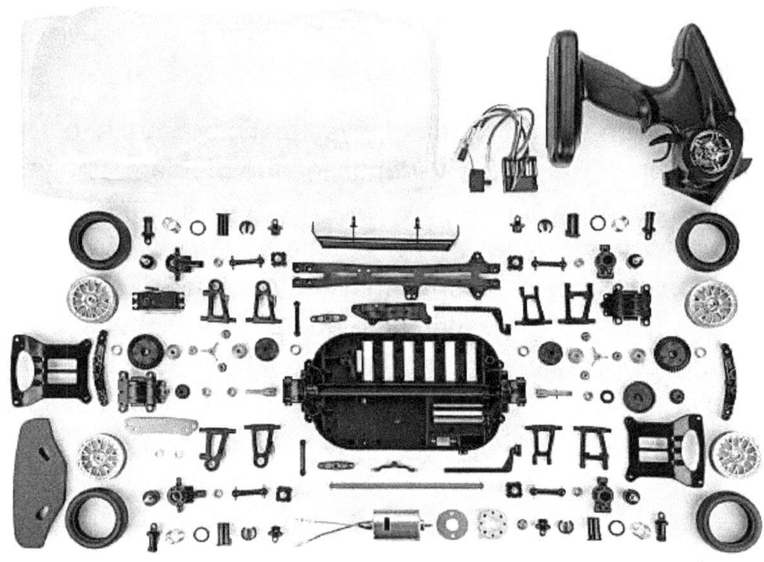

Repair Tools

Some recommended tools and equipment necessary for RC car repair are:

1. Screwdriver Set: A good quality screwdriver set with various sizes and types of screw heads is essential for disassembling and assembling parts.

2. Hex Key Set: Most RC cars use hex screws, so having a set of hex keys in different sizes will help you remove and tighten screws.

3. Pliers: Pliers are useful for gripping small parts, bending wires, and cutting zip ties or cables.

4. Needle Nose Pliers: These slim, pointed pliers allow access to tight areas and are handy for holding small parts or tightening screws in compact spaces.

5. Wire Cutters: Wire cutters are necessary for trimming and shaping wires during repairs or modifications.

6. Soldering Iron and Solder: If you plan to work on electronic components, a good soldering iron and solder are necessary for making and repairing connections.

7. Multimeter: A multimeter helps in diagnosing electrical issues by measuring voltage, continuity, and resistance.

8. Ball Joint Pliers: Ball joint pliers are designed to separate ball joints from the suspension, making it easier to replace or repair.

9. Shock Pliers: These specialized pliers are used to rebuild and maintain the shocks of an RC car.

10. Nut Driver Set: Nut drivers are useful for tightening and loosening nuts of various sizes found on different parts of the RC car.

11. Threadlock: Threadlock adhesive helps prevent screws from loosening due to vibrations during RC car operation.

12. Spare Parts: It's always a good idea to have some spare parts on hand, such as screws, gears, suspension parts, and other commonly replaced components.

13. Cleaning Supplies: A brush, compressed air, and a cleaning solution are helpful for removing dirt, debris, and grime from the RC car's internal and external parts.

Remember, the specific tools and equipment required may vary depending on the type and complexity of your RC car.

There are several brands and models that are highly recommended for advanced RC car repair tasks. Some of these include:

1. Team Losi: Known for their high-quality RC car models, Team Losi also produces a range of tools specifically designed for RC car repair, such as hex drivers, nut drivers, and pliers.

2. Dynamite: Dynamite offers a wide selection of RC car tools, including specialty tools like ball link pliers, shock shaft pliers, and turnbuckle wrenches.

3. Hudy: Hudy is a renowned brand in the RC car industry, and they provide a large number of precision tools for advanced RC car repair. Their tools are known for their high quality and durability.

4. ProTek RC: ProTek RC offers a range of tools designed specifically for RC car repair, including hex wrenches, nut drivers, and turnbuckle wrenches. They are known for their affordability and quality.

5. X-Acto: Although primarily known for their precision craft knives, X-Acto also produces a variety of tools useful for advanced RC car repair, such as razor saws, drill sets, and cutting mats.

It is important to note that the choice of brand or model ultimately depends on personal preference and budget. It is recommended to read reviews and gather feedback from other RC car enthusiasts before making a purchase.

Troubleshooting and fixing motor or electronic component failures in RC cars can be done by following these steps:

1. Identify the problem: Observe the RC car's behavior and identify the specific component that is not functioning correctly. It could be the motor, speed controller, receiver, transmitter, or any other electronic component.

2. Check the power source: Ensure that the battery is fully charged and connected properly. Verify that the power switch is in the correct position.

3. Inspect connections: Look for loose or disconnected wires, damaged connectors, or loose solder joints. Tighten any loose connectors and re-solder any damaged joints.

4. Check the motor: If the issue is with the motor, ensure that it spins freely and isn't jammed. Inspect the motor's wiring for any faults, and test the motor separately by connecting it directly to a power source (such as a battery) to check if it runs smoothly. If the motor doesn't operate properly, it may need to be replaced.

5. Test the speed controller: If the motor is fine, but not receiving proper power or commands, the issue could be with the speed controller. Check all the connections between the speed controller, receiver, and motor. Ensure that the speed controller is properly calibrated and programmed according to the RC car's requirements. If needed, reprogram or replace the speed controller.

6. Test the receiver and transmitter: Verify that the receiver is properly connected to both the speed controller and the transmitter. Check the batteries in the transmitter and replace them if necessary. If the car is not responding correctly to the transmitter's commands, try re-binding or reprogramming the receiver and transmitter.

7. Replace faulty components: If all the above steps fail to resolve the issue, it is possible that a component is faulty and needs to be replaced. In such cases, refer to the product manual or contact the manufacturer for guidance on replacement components.

Remember to always follow safety protocols while troubleshooting and fixing RC cars to avoid any accidents or damage to the vehicle. If you are inexperienced or uncertain about performing any repairs, it is recommended to seek assistance from an expert or consult a professional RC car technician

There are several suspension system modifications that have been made in RC cars to improve stability and reduce body roll during high-speed turns. Here are a few examples:

1. Stiffer Springs: By using stiffer suspension springs, the car's body roll can be reduced during high-speed turns. Stiffer springs provide increased resistance to weight transfer, keeping the chassis more level and improving stability.

2. Anti-Roll Bars: Anti-roll bars, also known as sway bars, are used to limit the amount of body roll during cornering. They connect the left and right suspension arms and provide additional resistance to body roll by transferring force from one side of the car to the other.

3. Lowering the Center of Gravity: Lowering the center of gravity helps reduce body roll by positioning the car's weight closer to the ground. This can be done by using a

lower ride height or installing lower profile tires. Lowering the center of gravity improves stability and responsiveness during high-speed turns.

4. Upgraded Dampers: High-quality dampers can help improve stability by providing better control over the suspension and reducing body roll. Adjustable dampers allow for fine-tuning the suspension to match different track conditions and driving styles.

5. Camber and Toe Adjustments: Fine-tuning the camber and toe settings of the wheels can also help improve stability during cornering. Negative camber (tilting the tires inward at the top) and toe-out (pointing the front tires slightly outward) can provide better cornering grip and reduce body roll.

6. Aerodynamic Upgrades: Some RC cars may feature aerodynamic enhancements such as spoilers or diffusers. These components help generate downforce, which pushes the car towards the ground, reducing body roll and increasing stability at high speeds.

Overall, these suspension system modifications are designed to enhance the car's stability, reduce body roll, and improve its overall handling during high-speed turns.

CONCLUSION

In conclusion, remote-controlled (RC) cars have become an increasingly popular hobby for people of all ages. The advancements in technology have allowed for greater precision, speed, and versatility in these miniature vehicles. Through this essay, we have seen how RC cars have evolved from simple toys to highly sophisticated machines, replicating real-life driving experiences. The introduction of different types of RC cars, such as on-road and off-road models, has widened the appeal of this hobby to a broader audience.

RC cars provide enthusiasts with an opportunity to engage in a thrilling and competitive activity. The ability to control these cars from a distance has added an element of excitement and skill development. Furthermore, the customization options available in the world of RC cars enable enthusiasts to personalize their vehicles, reflecting their unique styles and preferences.

Additionally, RC cars promote important skills such as hand-eye coordination, problem-solving, and creativity. This hobby requires precision and concentration to maneuver the cars effectively, enhancing motor skills and mental agility. Moreover, enthusiasts often engage in modifications and repairs, fostering problem-solving skills and a deeper understanding of mechanical systems.

Beyond the entertainment value, RC cars have also found applications in various industries. For instance, they are frequently utilized by engineers and automotive

designers to test prototypes and explore new techniques. This demonstrates the practical significance of RC cars in advancing technological advancements.

RC cars have come a long way from being simple toys. They now serve as a means of entertainment, skill development, and even as valuable tools in various industries. The future of RC cars appears promising, as technology continues to evolve, providing enthusiasts with even more advanced features and experiences. Whether one chooses to engage in the hobby for leisure or professional reasons, there is no doubt that RC cars have cemented their place in modern society.

www.ingramcontent.com/pod-product-compliance
Lightning Source LLC
Chambersburg PA
CBHW060758260726
48660CB00002B/682